DEVON
MOODS

LEE PENGELLY

HALSGROVE

First published in Great Britain in 2003

Title page photograph: *View of Sheepstor, Dartmoor*
Contents page photograph: *Moored boats on the River Tamar at Plymouth*

British Library Cataloguing-in-Publication Data
A CIP record for this title is available from the British Library

ISBN 1 84114 307 3

HALSGROVE
Halsgrove House
Lower Moor Way
Tiverton, Devon EX16 6SS
T: 01884 243242
F: 01884 243325

sales@halsgrove.com
www.halsgrove.com

Printed and bound
in Italy by D'Auria Industrie Grafiche Spa

CONTENTS

AUTHOR'S PREFACE

With its varied landscape of patchwork fields, broken hills, wild moorlands and dramatic coastlines it's not hard to see why Devon attracts so many visitors year after year. Whether you are travelling on one of the main routes through Devon or on one of the many country roads that criss-cross the county you can be sure that at every turn you will be greeted by either panoramic views, characterful buildings or grazing livestock.

Many of the photographs we see in books, magazines and on postcards and calenders repeatedly depict the more popular views and places in the region. However, there are many viewpoints which remain virtually undiscovered, magical corners that convey the character and history of the county. As a photographer I strive to capture these hidden places on film. Tiny details that tell a story and wide sweeping views that give a sense of space all combine to make a lasting record of our surroundings.

My aim in this book has been to compile a selection of these photographs which I hope reveal the true character of Devon. I have tried to include the familiar and unfamiliar but there are many places that I have yet to discover. I hope that this collection of images gives an insight into the county of Devon and inspires others to visit the places I have so much enjoyed capturing on film.

LEE PENGELLY
February, 2003

THE COAST

Smartly painted bathing huts stand sentinel on Paignton sea front.

Great Mew Stone sits in Wembury Bay, South Devon. The volcanic-looking island was once inhabited but is now the haven of seabirds.

Sunset over Wembury Bay and Great Mew Stone.

Bovisand Bay by evening light.

Lynmouth sea front sits below high cliffs, at the mercy of the East and West Lyn rivers which meet here, though now tamed by civil engineers since the flood disaster in August 1952.

*View from the cliff
railway that has
linked the 'twin
villages' of Lynton and
Lynmouth since their
Victorian heyday.*

St Helena's Church on Lundy was built for the Reverend Hudson Heaven, thus becoming known as the Kingdom of Heaven.

The picturesque harbour at Clovelly lies at the bottom of a steep cobbled street, and as you walk down between the houses there is the inescapable feeling of having stepped back in time. Well worth the walk down, and even the rather more testing pull up afterwards!

The revamped harbour at Exmouth.

*The Esplanade at Exmouth,
deserted under dramatic skies but
usually a popular tourist spot
with its wide sandy beach.*

The MS Oldenburg *leaves Lundy behind, shrouded in sea fog, as she heads back to Bideford.*

MS Oldenburg *arrives at Lundy landing platform with her cargo of tourists. Lundy, in the Bristol Channel, should never be called Lundy island – the name is Norse for 'puffin island'.*

*Cleaning the day's catch at the quayside
in Sutton Harbour, Plymouth.*

A *huge crab destined for one of Dartmouth's seafood restaurants.*

*Salcombe from
East Portlemouth.*

Fishing boats at Beer set beneath the high white cliffs of Beer Head.

The main line between
Penzance and London
Paddington snakes its way
around the Dawlish
coastline. At Coryton's
Cove the sea is only a
few metres away.

Seabirds on the Tamar estuary, Plymouth.

Cockwood Harbour,
near Starcross.

*Langstone Rock
at Dawlish.*

*An old ladder becomes
part of the landscape on
Dawlish Warren.*

TOWNS & VILLAGES

*Firework display over
Plymouth Sound.*

The Tamar road bridge and Brunel's railway bridge. The Royal Albert Bridge was Isambard Kingdom Brunel's last great achievement, spanning the River Tamar at a height of 100 feet with the total length of the bridge and its approaches at 2190 feet.

Smeaton's Tower,
Plymouth's well-known
landmark, was once the
Eddystone Lighthouse
and took up its home on
the Hoe in 1882. On a
clear day it can be seen
14 miles out at sea.

Drake's Island in Plymouth Sound was known as St Nicholas' Island until Sir Francis Drake was appointed governor and began to fortify it. Like Alcatraz, it was used as a prison for a time.

*Plympton St Maurice from Plympton Castle. One of four Devon Stannary towns, to which
tin mined on Dartmoor had to be taken, it is now an unspoilt and sleepy backwater.*

Buckland Abbey near Yelverton. The thirteenth-century Cistercian abbey later became the home of Sir Francis Drake.

Queen Anne's Walk at Barnstaple, a small stone arcade dating from 1609, was rebuilt in 1708.
It has a statue of Queen Anne upon its portico and was built as an exchange for the town's merchants.

The attractive town of Bideford sits alongside the river Torridge, spanned by a stout 24-arch bridge dating back to the fourteenth century.

Twinkling lights of Torbay at night.

Hesketh Crescent, Torquay, with its air of bygone elegance.

Monument to Lt Colonel William Morris at Hatherleigh. Morris led his regiment in the disastrous Charge of the Light Brigade at Balaclava in the Crimea. Though seriously injured, he was among the few survivors of the infamous military blunder, only to die years later from sunstroke.

A vibrantly painted trawler at Sutton Harbour, Plymouth.

Traditional Devon thatch at Old Mother Hubbard's restaurant, Yealmpton.

Cottages at Cockington, Torquay's traditional village within a town.

The creeper-covered Masons Arms at Branscombe.

Coombe Cottage at Branscombe. Adorned with a vivid display of flowers in spring and summer, it is always an eyecatching sight when you drive through the village.

The Talaton Inn, one of Devon's many country inns.

The Five Bells Inn
at Clyst Hydon
near Exeter.

Old petrol pumps at Talaton, reminiscent of a bygone age.

*Every spring time
vibrant clusters of
daffodils emerge adding
a touch of colour to
South Molton's parish
church green*

The early-twentieth-century Britannia Royal Naval College at Dartmouth makes a fine and imposing backdrop to the harbour below.

Bayards Cove at Dartmouth. This quaint quay with its seventeenth-century houses overlooks the Dart estuary.

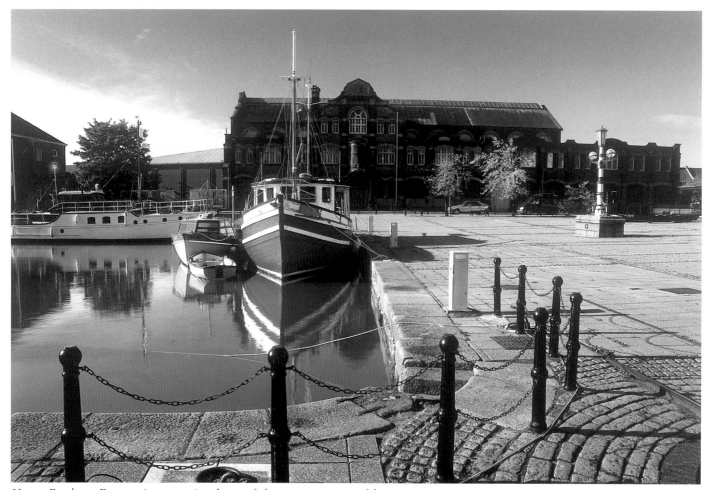

Haven Banks at Exeter. An attractive cluster of shops, restaurants and houses now sits alongside the main canal and former electricity generating station.

Exeter Quay bustles with tourists throughout the year. Its former warehouses and boathouses have a new life as shops, restaurants, cafés and bars along the water's edge where you can relax and watch swans feeding or more energetic human types rowing up and down the river.

Cathedral Close, Exeter. The perfect spot to escape the bustle of the city's main shopping streets and offices a stone's-throw away.

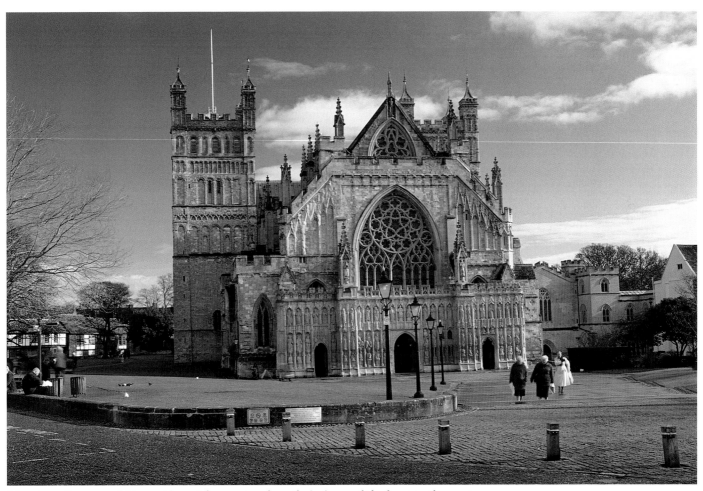

No trip to Exeter would be complete without seeing the cathedral, one of the finest in the country with its twin Norman towers, magnificent three-storey West Front with well-preserved statues, and inside 300 feet of unbroken vaulting weighing 5080 tonnes. A building to be proud of.

Moored boats on the misty Exe estuary at Topsham.

An old standpipe now provides a quirky feature in this Topsham garden.

The award-winning Miller's Crossing sits astride the River Exe in Exeter.

*Hot-air balloonists
all set for lift-off
near Exeter.*

The colonnaded granite almhouses at
Moretonhampstead which date from 1637.

Buckfastleigh Station, home of the
South Devon Railway or 'Primrose Line'.

*Swimbridge, North Devon,
from St James's churchyard
where Revd Jack Russell,
notable hunting parson and
breeder of the famous terrier,
is buried.*

*Fifteenth-century
St James's Church at
Swimbridge has a
fourteenth-century spire
and many fine features.*

Sheep grazing below Wembury church on the South Devon coast.

*Haldon Belvedere, Dunchideock. This fine folly was built in
1788 as a memorial to Major General Stringer Lawrence.*

*Wilderness Pond set
in the grounds of
Arlington Court,
North Devon.*

The Fisherman's Cot on the River Exe at Bickleigh in the heart of Devon.

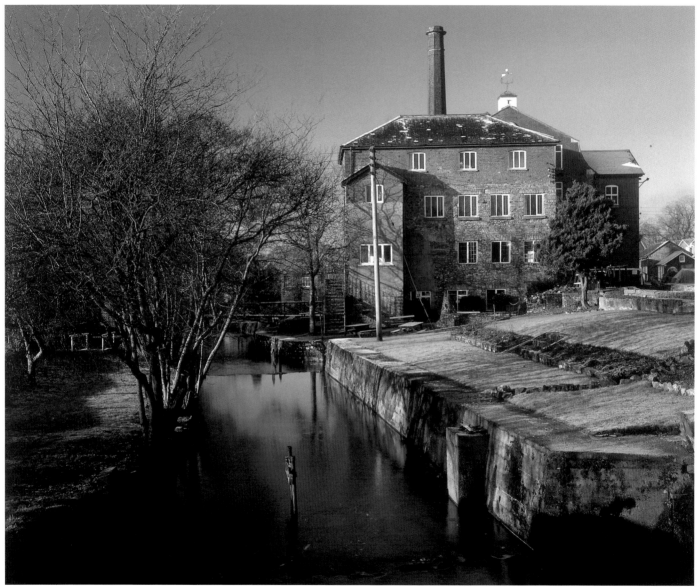

Coldharbour Mill, Uffculme, a wool mill until 1981, now a working museum.

Culmstock village sits either side of the river Culm,
spanned by a beautiful arched road bridge.

The fourteenth-century Rising Sun Hotel on Lynmouth's harbourside was once a haunt popular with smugglers.

The Mussel Inn at Down Thomas, South Devon.

Boats on the River Tamar near Cargreen.

Cottage ornée by the sea at Sidmouth, one of several examples of this rustic but Romantic architectural style to be found here.

Killerton House, Broadclyst, home to the Acland family for over three hundred years and rebuilt in 1778. Now National Trust owned, it houses a fascinating costume collection.

The parish church at Holsworthy catches the first rays of sun on a spring morning

The striking Landmark Theatre at Ilfracombe overlooking the bay.

A cormorant pauses on its fishing post on the River Dart at Totnes.

A rainbow frames Bicton Park Botanical Gardens near Budleigh Salterton. These beautiful grounds were laid out in 1735, after a design by Le Nôtre, designer of the elaborate gardens at the French palace of Versailles.

Harbertonford near Totnes, recently at the centre of the flood defence issue. Situated on the River Harbourne the village has suffered many devastating floods over the years.

The setting sun highlights the simple lines of St Helena Church on Lundy.

R U R A L   D E V O N

Staverton's quaint station, near Totnes,
has an air of being almost frozen in time.

Littlehempston church near Totnes.

Silverton Park was built as a palatial 187-room mansion in the mid-1800s but never completed. The stables, now owned by the Landmark Trust, are all that remain.

Radford ruins overlook Hooe Lake near Plymouth.

Mute swan enjoying the calm waters of a leat near Tiverton.

The mute swan, the commonest Eurasian swan, is a
a familiar and graceful sight on our waterways.

Rowing boats moored among the reed beds at Slapton Ley, the largest natural freshwater lake in Devon and an important haven for bird life.

Tidal road at Aveton Gifford.

A coot settles amongst a reed bed.

A tranquil River Taw reflects autumnal tints at Eggesford, North Devon.

A boat moored on the Harbourne river near Ashprington, South Devon.

A robin with its breakfast of insects in its beak.

A waterfall at Shaugh Prior, a favourite spot for many landscape artists.

*Dappled light brings
out the wonderful
textures of boulders on
the River Plym at
Shaugh Prior.*

A buttercup-filled meadow at Creacombe, Yealmpton.

Grazing cattle at Rix Farm near Tiverton.

*The Tarka Trail
near Weare Giffard,
North Devon.*

A buzzard scans its feeding grounds from a roadside post at Postbridge on Dartmoor.

A herd of fallow deer at the Dartmoor Wildlife Park, Sparkwell.

The timeless beauty of bluebells and buttercups in a spring meadow.

Shaugh Bridge spans the River Plym at one end of a beautiful walk through Plym Bridge Woods to the edge of the Dartmoor National Park.

*Tin-work ruins,
Shaugh Prior.*

*Water rushes over
Plymbridge weir.*

*Though Burrator Reservoir on Dartmoor's western fringe is
a popular tourist spot, solitude can still be found nearby.*

A sow and her piglets try to find some shade from the sun on a Totnes farm.

Typically Devonian, a rusting tractor, rolling farmland and bluebells. One of those stumbled-upon scenes at South Zeal.

A leafy pathway leads off into the autumnal woods at Plymbridge.

A misty morning at Umberleigh in the Taw Valley, near South Molton.

Autumn woodland glows in the mid-morning sun.

*Grazing sheep under
a stormy sky at
Bratton Clovelly,
near Okehampton.*

The River Yeo near Morchard Bishop, mid Devon.

Foxgloves carpet the forest floor at Berry Pomeroy, near Totnes.

Gull in winter sunset over the Tamar estuary.

*A wintry scene on the edge of the moors near Okehampton;
snowfall comes and goes within days.*

Maize crop at Rix Farm, Tiverton.

DARTMOOR
HEART OF DEVON

Clapper bridge at Postbridge. The best known bridge of this type,
spanning the East Dart river, it is the largest clapper on the moor
at over 40 feet in length. The newer road bridge stands alongside.

*Newleycombe
Lake which runs
down into Burrator
Reservoir.*

*Arboretum lake
at Burrator.*

Burrator Reservoir, whose construction caused great controversy and displacement of local families, has supplied Plymouth and other nearby towns with their water since 1898.

Newleycombe Lake is one of Dartmoor's many fast-flowing streams.

*Powder Mills at Postbridge. The remains of a gunpowder
factory opened in 1844 by George Frean.*

*The church of
St Michael de Rupe on
Brent Tor, with storm clouds
scudding in from the west.
Dating from c.1150 the
church stands at over 1100
feet above sea level.*

Leather Tor dominates the skyline above Burrator Reservoir.

*Another view of
Leather Tor*

A wind-battered tree bathed in moonlight at Sheepstor.

*Dartmoor ponies graze
near Princetown.*

Brent Tor church sits atop a 1130ft-high volcanic outcrop near Tavistock. According to legend the twelfth-century church of St Michael was built by a grateful merchant whose ship had narrowly escaped shipwreck. However, it is likely that monks from Tavistock Abbey were responsible its founding.

Princetown church tower stands like a beacon in the bleak landscape.

Sunset over Meavy.

The River Dart at Dartmeet.

A small stream turns into a waterfall in the Dart Valley.

*Looking across to Okehampton. The town was mentioned
in the Domesday book and was one of only two market
towns in the country at the time of the Norman conquest.*

The unpredictable Dartmoor weather can change from glorious sunshine to violent storms in a matter of hours.

View of Lydford from Brat Tor.

Okehampton Castle is one of the best preserved castles in the west country, dating from the eleventh century.

Merrivale stone row.

*Bleak House ruins
near Lydford.*

Vixen Tor.

Wheal Betsy near Tavistock was worked for tin periodically in the nineteenth century until 1870. The disused engine house is now owned by the National Trust.

Bennett's Cross overlooking Headland Warren near Postbridge. The medieval cross marked an ancient track over the moor.

*Dartmoor ponies
grazing near Black
Tor on Dartmoor.*

Silhouette of Leeden Tor against the evening sky.